SELF DISCOVERY
JOURNAL

122 Thought Provoking Questions

Lydell M. King

authorHOUSE®

AuthorHouse™
1663 Liberty Drive
Bloomington, IN 47403
www.authorhouse.com
Phone: 833-262-8899

Published by AuthorHouse 06/25/2022

ISBN: 978-1-6655-6265-2 (sc)
ISBN: 978-1-6655-6264-5 (e)

Print information available on the last page.

Any people depicted in stock imagery provided by Getty Images are models,
and such images are being used for illustrative purposes only.
Certain stock imagery © Getty Images.

This book is printed on acid-free paper.

CONTENTS

- PROLOGUE -

LET ME FIRST SAY TO YOU! THE READER, THANK YOU FOR TAKING THIS JOURNEY WITH ME, BY READING THESE THOUGHT PROVOKING QUESTIONS! AS YOU WILL SEE, I LAY OUT THE QUESTION AND ANSWER THE QUESTIONS SO YOU CAN GET TO KNOW, AND HAVE A BETTER UNDERSTANDING ABOUT MYSELF AND THROUGH THIS, I WANT TO CHALLENGE YOU TO USE THIS AS A JOURNAL, SO YOU CAN LEARN MORE ABOUT YOURSELF, AS WELL. IN DOING THIS, YOU NEVER KNOW! YOU MIGHT WANT TO WRITE A BOOK OR JUST USE THIS TO GET YOUR THOUGHTS OUT. WHEN WE SET OUR MIND ON SOME THEN, MOST OF THE TIME GOOD THINGS HAPPEN. LIFE IS ABOUT LIVING, AND LEARNING, AND SHARING WHAT YOU HAVE LEARNED WITH OTHERS. MY HOPE AS YOU TAKE THIS JOURNEY, AND READ THESE THOUGHT PROVOKING QUESTIONS, THESE QUESTIONS WILL HELP YOU HAVE A MUCH BETTER UNDERSTANDING ABOUT WHO YOU ARE, AND WHAT YOU HAVE TO OFFER THE WORLD! WE ALL HAVE A PURPOSE, IT'S UP TO US TO FIND OUT WHAT THIS PURPOSE IS. ONE OF THE GOOD THINGS ABOUT THIS BOOK, AND THESE QUESTIONS IS, AS YOU READ, AND THINK ABOUT THESE QUESTIONS. THE ANSWER YOU GIVE TODAY, MAY NOT BE THE ANSWER YOU WRITE DOWN A YEAR FROM NOW. THESE QUESTIONS FIND YOU IN THE MIND SET NOW, AND HELP YOU THINK, AND PLAN FOR THE FUTURE. GROWTH IS BEAUTIFUL, ALL LIFE HAS A PURPOSE. WHAT IS YOUR?

-THE UNFORGOTTEN-

THANK YOU ALL THAT HAS NEVER GIVEN UP ON ME.
IT'S YOUR FIRE THAT KEEPS ME GOING, KEEPS
ME WANTING TO BE BETTER EACH, AND EVERY DAY.
LIFE CAN BE CRUEL, AND NOT UNDERSTANDING.
THROUGH MY LIFE BATTLES, I HAVE OVER COME
WHAT MOST WOULD HAVE LOST THEIR WAY,
HOWEVER WITH THOSE THAT LOVE ME,
AND JUST WANTED BETTER FOR ME, THANK YOU ALL.
I CONTINUE TO DO ONTO THOSE
WHAT I WANT DONE ONTO ME,
THIS IS TO BE UNDERSTOOD, AND REMEMBERED
FOR THE GOOD I DO. LIFE IS A BLESSING. THANK YOU.

QUESTION 1.

(Who Are You?)

I am a man that was born with the name Lydell Marcus white, and as I got older and I found myself. I changed my name to Lydell Eehmah King. In my eyes this is giving me a new start at life. My past is behind me, my past struggles and my gains has made me into the man I am today. Life offers up all kinds of challenges, it's how you bounce back from them down falls which make you into the person that you are seeking to be.

_____

_____

_____

_____

_____

_____

_____

_____

_____

_____

_____

_____

_____

_____

_____

_____

_____

_____

QUESTION 2.

(Write Something About Yourself)

I am a very strong minded man, that has been locked up since I was 15 years old, I have not allowed this time to make me bitter, however I have continued to learn from every body around me, learn from their mistakes. I understand their gains as well. Life is a thinking game, as long as you take your time and think before you move, you will be good. I think this is why I love playing the game chess so much, because it's a thinking game. I try and make sure that I pass all the knowledge that I have down to my daughter and my gran daughters. They are our family future.

_____

_____

_____

_____

_____

_____

_____

_____

_____

_____

_____

_____

_____

_____

QUESTION 3.

(What are The Things That Make You The Happiest?)

One of the things that make me the happiest is when I hear my daughter call me dad, because all my life, I wanted to be a better father then I had. Be that very outgoing gran father that god wanted me to be. As a kid I remember just wanting to make my mother happy. Now when I see my mother happy this makes me happy. Seeing and making those that I love happy, makes me feel worthy of happiness.

_____

_____

_____

_____

_____

_____

_____

_____

_____

_____

_____

_____

_____

_____

_____

_____

_____

_____

QUESTION 4.

(What Are The Things That Worry You The Most?)

The number one thing that worries me the most is making sure that I get out of prison before my mother has any major issues with her health. t have seen to many people here in prison who has lost their parents, and I pray every day that is not me. My heart goes out to those that has to deal with loosing a parent or just a family member.

_____

_____

_____

_____

_____

_____

_____

_____

_____

_____

_____

_____

_____

_____

_____

_____

_____

_____

QUESTION 5.

(Would You Still Work If You Won The Lottery?)

If I won the lottery, I would still work, because I was raised to work, and if I'm not working I feel like I'm worthless. Now that I'm older I would invest in my money, make sure that I'm doing good with it. I would create a space where I could teach those that want to learn more about how to make things work for you, just be that good support for my community.

QUESTION 6.

(Write About The Single Person You Love The Most?)

This is a very good, thought provoking question, when I first put this question together. My first thought, and answer to this question would be my twin brother. Then I put more thought into it. It would go in this order. God for giving my mother the ability to give birth to my twin and l. My mother for having us, and giving us her all Even though we did not make it easy on her. Then my twin brother, for being there when nobody else was. I can truly say, without my twin brother, my other half, there would have been many struggling days by myself. I know my answer is more then one, however there is not just one person that I love the most.

_____

_____

_____

_____

_____

_____

_____

_____

_____

_____

_____

_____

_____

QUESTION 7.

(Write Something About The Most Important People In Your Life.)

I feel like, god has allowed every body to come, and go out of my life, so I can learn, good and bad things. The people that has been in my life for the last 20 plus years, through the good and bad things, these are the most important people in my life.

_____

_____

_____

_____

_____

_____

_____

_____

_____

_____

_____

_____

_____

_____

_____

_____

_____

_____

QUESTION 8.

(What Do You Like Doing The Most?)

There are two things I like doing the most. One, I love helping people in all kinds of ways, when I do this, I feel like I am doing my part, and what I was put on this earth to do. Two, I love doing hair, and it's something that I have like doing. It's something about doing some ones hair and seeing them feel good about them self and me knowing that I had a hand in making them feel good.

_____

_____

_____

_____

_____

_____

_____

_____

_____

_____

_____

_____

_____

_____

_____

_____

QUESTION 9.

(What Do You Like and Dislike About Your Parents?)

My father had a lot of creations, he is very smart, however he also made a lot of dumb mistakes, I dislike that my father made so many mistakes and did not learn from them as he moved on in his life. My mother, I like that my mom has taught me all of my family morals, and how to be the best man I can be, never give up no matter what life through at you. What I dislike about my mother is I don't like that my mom don't take care of herself the best however I know if I was there, things would be different.

QUESTION 10.

(If You Had A Chance, Would You Change Your Partner For Another One?)

Being a single person I would look to cultivating a friendship first and foremost with someone that is mentally and emotionally available self-sufficient and someone with the potential to grow/partner with.

_____

_____

_____

_____

_____

_____

_____

_____

_____

_____

_____

_____

_____

_____

_____

_____

_____

_____

QUESTION 11.

(What Do You Like The Most And Hate About Your Partner?)

What I liked about my ex wife is, in the beginning she really had a lot of faith in me, and us as a team. Then she allowed her past to come between us and her faith in me. Once the faith and trust is gone, the relationship won't work.

_____

_____

_____

_____

_____

_____

_____

_____

_____

_____

_____

_____

_____

_____

_____

_____

_____

_____

QUESTION 12.

(Do You Like Your Job?)

I currently work in the infirmary here at the prison, and I must say that this is one of the best jobs that I have ever had. Having this job has given me the chance to help those that are not able to help them self. Having this job gives me the chance to give back, and have some sense of self worth.

_____

_____

_____

_____

_____

_____

_____

_____

_____

_____

_____

_____

_____

_____

_____

_____

_____

_____

_____

QUESTION 13.

(Do You Believe In God?)

I believe in god, however I don't believe in picking a religion. I have read a lot of books on all of the religions and most of them say the same things. I know that we all have come from somewhere, so I pray to the higher power, god! Each and every day.

QUESTION 14.

(What Makes You Smile?)

A lot of things makes me smile. When I know that I do something that makes people smile, I smile. Because I feel like that we all should smile and make others smile as well. When I wake up every day, and I am able to walk, talk, see and just be the best me each, and every day, this makes me smile because there are a lot of people that can't say this.

QUESTION 15.

(Have You Hurt Anyone?)

Yes, I have and on more then one level, I am not proud of my past actions, however I can and will say this. I have learned from my actions and this allows me to want to be better. Because if you are not continuing to grow and be better, then what is the purpose of living?

QUESTION 16.

(What's The Single Most Outrageous Thing You Have Ever Done?)

The single most outrageous thing that I have ever done. I remember when my twin brother and I was younger, we use to act like each other with our girlfriends so we could share. The pluses of being a twin!

_____

_____

_____

_____

_____

_____

_____

_____

_____

_____

_____

_____

_____

_____

_____

_____

_____

QUESTION 17.

(Is There Anything That You Are Scared Of?)

There are a few things that I am scared of, like the first one is, I am scared of loosing my mother before I get out of prison. Two, I'm scared of snakes, and this started when I was young, like when I was like 12 or 13 years old. Then the last one is, I'm scared to fail, like I know we all fail, but I'm talking about failing to the point where I'm not able to bounce back from.

_____

_____

_____

_____

_____

_____

_____

_____

_____

_____

_____

_____

_____

_____

_____

_____

_____

QUESTION 18.

(What Is That One Thing That Matters To You The Most And Why?)

Family is what matters the most to me. Because without family, you have nothing, and if you have nothing then you are just here. Family can come in all kinds of forms, family can come from close friends or strong co workers.

_____

_____

_____

_____

_____

_____

_____

_____

_____

_____

_____

_____

_____

_____

_____

_____

_____

_____

QUESTION 19.

(Have You Done Anything Recently To Make Someone Smile?)

I try, and make people smile each and every day, life is about bettering those around you. I consider myself to be a joking type of person, so I'm always trying to put a smile on peoples faces.

QUESTION 20.

(How Long Do You Want To Live And Why?)

I want to live as long as I can, I don't want to live and be in pain. However I do want to live long enough to leave a good mark on this each, and my loved ones.

QUESTION 21.

(If You Could Change The Laws Would You And Why?)

Yes, I would if I was in the position to do so. I'm currently working on changing the laws on how Oregon deals with their juveniles in the state of Oregon, and how their sentence juveniles as well. I was 15 years old when I made a big mistake and the state of OREGON gave me 66 years for my crime, and 26 years later, I am just now winning in the courts and giving the state of Oregon the time they gave me back, and changing the laws in the process.

_____

_____

_____

_____

_____

_____

_____

_____

_____

_____

_____

_____

_____

_____

_____

_____

_____

QUESTION 22.

(What Is Worse: Never Trying Or Trying But Failing Many Times?)

I think never trying would be worse, because when you don't try, you are leaving the door open to a lot of "what if's!" and with trying, and failing many times, you giving yourself the chance to learn from your mistakes and gain knowledge of what to do better next time many times over.

_____

_____

_____

_____

_____

_____

_____

_____

_____

_____

_____

_____

_____

_____

_____

_____

_____

_____

QUESTION 23.

(What Is The Worst Thing That Has Ever Happened To You?)

The worst thing that has ever happened to me is, my father left our house, and from this action I developed abandonment issues. These abandonment issues drove me to do my crime in which brought me to prison. From there my beautiful daughter had to grow up without a father, repeating the cycle of black fathers not being there for their kids and filling up all of the prisons.

The sick cycle of my male family tree of men being locked up ends with me. From this point on, I will do everything in my power to change the family cycle.

QUESTION 24.

(What Is The Worst Thing You Have Ever Done)

The worst thing that I have ever done is what I did to come to prison. I took two peoples lives, and this is something that will stick with me for the rest of my life. This is why I strive every day to be better than I was yesterday. Yes, I did a big wrong, however I will not allow my actions as a kid to define who I am now, but it will make me better then who I was.

_____

_____

_____

_____

_____

_____

_____

_____

_____

_____

_____

_____

_____

_____

_____

_____

_____

_____

QUESTION 25.

(What Is The Best Thing That Has Ever Happened To You?)

The best thing that has ever happened to me is, I was born a twin with a very beautiful mother, then I had a beautiful daughter that blessed me with two smart, beautiful gran daughters that I will be able to pass down all of my knowledge and love too.

QUESTION 26.

(Are You Happy With Your Body?)

I will say that I'm not fully happy with my body because I want to be just a little bit bigger, and little more cut up.

_____

_____

_____

_____

_____

_____

_____

_____

_____

_____

_____

_____

_____

_____

_____

_____

_____

_____

_____

QUESTION 27.

(What Would You Change About Your Personality?)

As I sit here and think about this Question, I don't think that I would change anything about my personality. Now at times I can over think things, get into my own head at times, however I would not change my personality.

QUESTION 28.

(Do People Like You?)

I would like to believe that people like me. know the people that start off not liking me for whatever reason, once they get to know me they will grow to like me. I am a very outgoing person, I have make some very bad choices in life, however a lot of people have, I have made it my life's work to be better every day, and I want to make every body that I come in contact with better them they where before we met.

_____

_____

_____

_____

_____

_____

_____

_____

_____

_____

_____

_____

_____

_____

_____

_____

_____

QUESTION 29.

(Do You Like Yourself, Why And Why Not?)

For a long time, I could not forgive myself for what I did to come to prison. Then I learned 10 years into my sentence that in order to truly love someone, I First have to forgive myself, then I open the door to grow, and I'm able to give my all to the people that I love, and that love me.

_____

_____

_____

_____

_____

_____

_____

_____

_____

_____

_____

_____

_____

_____

_____

_____

_____

_____

QUESTION 30.

(What Do You Think Your Life Would Be Like 10 Years From Now?)

10 years from now I'm working on making sure that I have my hair shop up and running. I will be doing speaking engagements where I will be talking to troubled youth, telling my story so I can help others so they don't have to go down the road that I have.

QUESTION 31.

(Which One Of Your Friends Would You Like Me To Meet?)

I would like for you to meet my twin brother, Laycelle, because he is very down to earth. He will have you thinking. Plus this is my brother, my other half of me, we where born a minute apart from each other, and most of the time we can feel each other, and know what each other are thinking just by a look we give each other. Most people get a kick out of watching each other, this is my best friend.

QUESTION 32.

(What Kind Of People Do You Like?)

The people that I like are people that like to speak their mind, people that's not scared to stand on what they believe in. loyal people, when you are loyal, you put what you expect back. Lead by example. My mom has always told me, you treat people like you want to be treated. You do good things, and good things will come your way.

QUESTION 33.

(What Would You Do If You Were Famous?)

I would step up and be the voice for those that can't talk or that don't know how. We have a lot of people in the world that need help in a lot of ways, I would use me being famous to bring up topics that need to be talked about and brought to the forefront, I want to be the voice for the people.

QUESTION 34.

(Have You Ever Given To Charity? Why Or Why Not?)

Yes, I have given charity. Because I believe, "you do onto those that you want done onto you." If you give out good energy, you will get that good energy back.

QUESTION 35.

(If You Were To Be Reborn Again, What Would You Like To Be Reborn As?)

I would like to be reborn as a younger man, so this wiry, I can have all the knowledge that I do now, and being younger, I would do all positive things, so I can change the outlook that the world has on juveniles that make a mistake. Restore that hope in our youth that has been lost.

QUESTION 36.

(Is There One Thing That You Want Most Out Of Life?)

The thing that I want most out of life, is to be loved like I love. I want my life to have strong purpose.

_____

_____

_____

_____

_____

_____

_____

_____

_____

_____

_____

_____

_____

_____

_____

_____

_____

_____

_____

_____

_____

QUESTION 37.

(How Would You Like To Be Remembered?)

I want to be remembered as the man that got locked as a kid, a 15 year old kid, and through the 20 plus years, he made many mistakes, however he overcame them, went on to write 4 books, do many speaking panels where he loved speaking to troubled youth, and the people that take care of them. I just want to be remembered for the positive impact that I had on people that really know me.

_____

_____

_____

_____

_____

_____

_____

_____

_____

_____

_____

_____

_____

_____

_____

_____

_____

_____

_____

_____

QUESTION 38.

(If You Were To Get Cancer And Had 6 Months To Live, What Would You Do And How Would You Live Your Last Days Of Your Life?)

My answer comes from where I'm at now in my life. If I had cancer, and only had 5 months to live, I would spend my last 6 months on this earth fixing all the pain that I have brought upon this earth. I would do everything in my power to leave a good, positive mark on peoples lives. Let people know that we all have a purpose, we just have to seek it out. I would spend my last days with people that love me.

_____

_____

_____

_____

_____

_____

_____

_____

_____

_____

_____

_____

_____

_____

_____

_____

_____

QUESTION 39.

(What Is Your Worst Nightmare?)

My worst nightmare is, I have been locked up for the last 26 years, and I have watched so many people loose their parents while they are in prison, and I don't want to ever go through that.

_____

_____

_____

_____

_____

_____

_____

_____

_____

_____

_____

_____

_____

_____

_____

_____

_____

_____

_____

QUESTION 40.

(How Would You Like To Die?)

I would like to die fast, like in my sleep. I don't want to die in pain or slow. I work here in the infirmary at this prison, and I see people die slow all the time, and this is hard on these guys family's, and it's very slow on the guy that's dyeing. t want my family and friends to remember me Iooking healthy as can be.

QUESTION 41.

(What Does Success Actually Mean To You?)

Success to me means, when you are able to touch people lives in a positive way. When these same people hear or read your name, they light up because you have left a good imprint on them, you have meaning to them.

_____

_____

_____

_____

_____

_____

_____

_____

_____

_____

_____

_____

_____

_____

_____

_____

_____

_____

_____

_____

QUESTION 42.

(How Do You Spend Your Free Time?)

I spend my free time reading a book, watching a knowledgeable W program, I believe in "teach one reach one."

_____

_____

_____

_____

_____

_____

_____

_____

_____

_____

_____

_____

_____

_____

_____

_____

_____

_____

_____

_____

QUESTION 43.

(One Place That You Would Like To Travel To And Why?)

I would like to travel to Africa, because I have heard from all the people that have been there that once they get off the plane, and they touch down there, they can feel the spirits of the people and the history of the land. I want a chance to feel what that's like.

_____

_____

_____

_____

_____

_____

_____

_____

_____

_____

_____

_____

_____

_____

_____

_____

_____

_____

_____

_____

QUESTION 44.

(Which Bad Habits Would You Like To Get Rid Of?)

I sometimes pre judge people if they don't look at or deal with issues as I do. I don't like conflict, so I find a way to fix the situation. I live my life on my morals, and my family code, now most of the time if people don't line up with this then most likely I don't go out my way to talk to them.

QUESTION 45.

(Take Yourself 10 Years Back, What Would You Like To Change About Your Life?)

I would change that so many of my family members has passed sense I have been locked up. Then I would change me getting married, because I know, and understand that it's a lot of work and if one person is doing all the work then it's not going to work.

QUESTION 46.

(What Are Your Goals In Life?)

I have many reachable goals that I have been working on and have in motion. However my biggest one that I look forward to doing is, with all that I do positive, I want to reach, and touch as many people as I can. I now truly understand my worth, I want to show people that if I can do and overcome things so can they. Never give up, continue to fight.

_____

_____

_____

_____

_____

_____

_____

_____

_____

_____

_____

_____

_____

_____

_____

_____

_____

QUESTION 47.

(How Do You Plan To Achieve Your Goals?)

Continue doing what I have. I talk to people that's on the same path that I am. I talk to those that wish to have their own business, and that already have their own business as well. I believe "if you want to do good, and thrive in life, you have to be around those that's thriving in life already."

QUESTION 48.

(What Do You Want The Most In Life?)

What I want the most in life, is to be remembered for being the best son, brother, father, and gran father I could. The one that brought joy to peoples faces. Just was a all round good person. I want to be one of them people that someone can pick up something that I have wrote, and said, and they can see the joy that I put into my work.

QUESTION 49.

(What Inspires You The Most?)

ls when I can truly see the impacted on other peoples lives. I now have a positive voice where people listen, and l want to make sure that l take full advantage of this. I will continue to tell my story, and show we "we all have purpose."

QUESTION 50.

(Is There Something That No One Knows About You Other Than Yourself?)

When t have conflicts with people, my first thought is always the worst. Everything I do, I challenge myself, this is how I push myself to be better, and go to levels that most people won't.

_____

_____

_____

_____

_____

_____

_____

_____

_____

_____

_____

_____

_____

_____

_____

_____

_____

_____

_____

QUESTION 51.

(If You Had To Make One Minute Speech To The World, What Would You Say?)

I would spend the one minute saying, we as a nation of people have spent too much time hating, and giving up on each other, we need to take a little more time, and try to understand we as a people say, and do the things we do. It's easy to hate what we don't understand or like.

_____

_____

_____

_____

_____

_____

_____

_____

_____

_____

_____

_____

_____

_____

_____

_____

_____

_____

QUESTION 52.

(So Far In Life, What Do You Regret The Most?)

I regret that I as a kid, committed a crime with the motive to follow after a man! My father! Seeking the lost, the void that I had in my life at that time, and in doing this, my daughter lost out on me being there for her as she Brew up.

_____

_____

_____

_____

_____

_____

_____

_____

_____

_____

_____

_____

_____

_____

_____

_____

_____

QUESTION 53.

(What Are You Most Proud Of?)

I'm most proud of my daughter not turning out like her mother, and I. I'm proud that she is much better at a lot them her mother, and I'm proud that I am able to put my thoughts to words for the world to read. I'm most proud of my mother for being the back bone for everybody. She has been through so much in this world, "we all are blessing to be found."

_____
_____
_____
_____
_____
_____
_____
_____
_____
_____
_____
_____
_____
_____
_____
_____
_____

QUESTION 54.

(Are You Afraid Of Dying?)

I'm not afraid of dying, what I'm afraid of is, when I die, I won't have all the things together to make sure my loved once are okay.

QUESTION 55.

(Can You Spend 1 Week Alone On An Island?)

Yes, I could spend a week alone on an island, in that one week, I would journey through the island, taking in all that I could, and learn as much as I could in a week.

QUESTION 56.

(Do You Openly Talk About Your Feelings Or Do You Keep Them To Your Self?)

When I was younger, I did not talk about my feelings, because I did not know how to express my feelings. So I kept them inside. Now that I'm older, I'm able to express my feelings the right way, and be clear about what I'm trying to say.

_____

_____

_____

_____

_____

_____

_____

_____

_____

_____

_____

_____

_____

_____

_____

_____

_____

_____

QUESTION 57.

(Is There Someone You Wish Were Dead?)

I truly understand the value of life, human life, I don't wish nobody death, life is to preaches to wish this. I also believe in karma, like my mom would always say. "you do onto those that you want done onto you." This has stuck with me, and I want to pass this onto you.

QUESTION 58.

(What Is Your Ideal Self?)

My ideal self is some one that's strong in more then one way. Some one that brings the good out in people. Some one that's a leader, and most people don't mind following behind because they know this person would not ask something that he or she would not do them self.

_____

_____

_____

_____

_____

_____

_____

_____

_____

_____

_____

_____

_____

_____

_____

_____

_____

_____

QUESTION 59.

(Are You Living The Life Of Your Dreams?)

No I'm not living my life, l won't be until lam able to sit down with a big group of troubled youth, and tell my story. So they can see that they can overcome anything. Show them that I once wanted to give up, but I did not and I am here talking to them now.

QUESTION 60.

(Do You Have A Dream That You Would Like To Be Fulfilled?)

My dream that I would like to be fulfilled is, I want to be known for all the writings, and books I have done and how I have touched, and helped changed a lot of peoples lives.

QUESTION 61.

(What Are The Top Priorities Of Your Life Right Now?)

One of my top priorities in my life right now, is to make sure that I see my freedom again before my mom loose her health to bad. Another top priority of mine is to get out, and be the best father that I can, and be the best gram father as well.

QUESTION 62.

(Do You Wish You Had A Better House, Better Car And More Money?)

Seeing that I not currently living in a house, I don't have a car, however I do wish that I had more money. With more money comes that nice house that I want, with more money I will be able to invest in the things that I need, and not the things that I want.

QUESTION 63.

(What Is Your Favorite Food?)

I'm a very picky eater, and I can say! I'm not a really big sea food eater. My favorite food is chicken, or chicken strips, chicken nuggets, and I'm a fan of pizza as well.

QUESTION 64.

(What Good Habits You Would Have Liked To Have?)

I believe that it is never too late to build good or bad habits, I believe if you want good habits then you will work on have better habits then what you currently have. This goes for the bad habits as well.

_____

_____

_____

_____

_____

_____

_____

_____

_____

_____

_____

_____

_____

_____

_____

_____

_____

_____

_____

QUESTION 65.

(What TV Programs Do You Like Watching The Most And Why?)

I love building off the grid, Game of Thrones, Power, anything where you can learn and gain more knowledge then you had before.

QUESTION 66.

(Are You Jealous Of Anyone And Why?)

I can truly say I'm not jealous of any body, I will say, I'm envy of people living their best life. I haven't had the chance to live my best life, and when I do, I will make sure that everything that I do, I will make it count.

_____

_____

_____

_____

_____

_____

_____

_____

_____

_____

_____

_____

_____

_____

_____

_____

_____

_____

QUESTION 67.

(How Do You Express Your Anger?)

When I was younger, I would take my anger out on all the wrong people, and that put me in a lot of bad situations, now that I'm older. I like to work out. Working out is a very good way to let off the anger that's inside.

_____

_____

_____

_____

_____

_____

_____

_____

_____

_____

_____

_____

_____

_____

_____

_____

_____

_____

_____

_____

_____

QUESTION 68.

(Are You A Good Person?)

I would like to think that I'm a good person. I feel like, being a good person is not defined by some one saying that you are a good person, however, by what you do, and if it comes from the heart. Good people do things because they want to, not because they have to.

QUESTION 69.

(If You Were Given 3 Wishes, What Would You Ask For?)

My first wish would be to be the 10th richest person on earth, so I could help change the community in anyway is needed. My second wish, I would be something like a Jessie Jackson, a voice for the people, the juveniles around the world. Now my last wish would be to change the prison system, and how they deal with people of color. We make up for a lot of the population in most of the states, things have to change!

QUESTION 70.

(If You Had More Money Would You Be Happier?)

I can't say that I would be happier, however I will say that I would be more set that I have the money, this will be one less thing that I would have to worry about.

_____

_____

_____

_____

_____

_____

_____

_____

_____

_____

_____

_____

_____

_____

_____

_____

_____

_____

_____

QUESTION 71.

(If Money Was No Issue, Where Would You Live And Why?)

I would buy my own island, 3rd of the island would be fruit tree's, peanut plants, so when I didn't feel like leaving the island I would be good.

_____

_____

_____

_____

_____

_____

_____

_____

_____

_____

_____

_____

_____

_____

_____

_____

_____

_____

_____

_____

_____

_____

QUESTION 72.

(What Is Your Favorite Song And Why Do You Like It?)

I really don't have a favorite song, I go off of my mood for the day. Like when I working out, I go for rap songs that will get me ready to work out, get my blood rennin. Then when I'm on my romantic side then I like to listen to R&B. Like Silk, Trey songs, Isley Brothers.

QUESTION 73.

(Who Do You Admire The Most And Why?)

The people that has been through so much, and they keep going, and never give up. They have made the situation that they have went through to make them a much better person, and that has shinned off onto other people. This is who I admire the most.

_____

_____

_____

_____

_____

_____

_____

_____

_____

_____

_____

_____

_____

_____

_____

_____

_____

_____

_____

QUESTION 74.

(What is The Biggest Lie You Have Ever Told?)

I use to lie about what I did that brought me to prison, because I did not want people to judge me from my past because that's not who I am today.

_____

_____

_____

_____

_____

_____

_____

_____

_____

_____

_____

_____

_____

_____

_____

_____

_____

_____

_____

QUESTION 75.

(Is There Anything That You Feel Guilty About?)

No I don't feel guilty about anything, I have no problem speaking my mind, and putting my all into fixing my wrongs. If I was to feel guilty about anything, it would be, all the wrongs I have done. I wake up every day, working on fixing my wrongs.

QUESTION 76.

(If You Could Pick One Family Member Or Mentor That You Grew Up Knowing, Now Look Up To, Who Would That Be, How Did They Influence You?)

The one family member that I grew up knowing, and now look up to, is my mom. I have been locked up for most of my life, and my mom has been my rock, the one person that has been strong, and I look to her for a lot of answers. My mom has influenced me by the knowledge she has passed down to, and continues to do.

_____

_____

_____

_____

_____

_____

_____

_____

_____

_____

_____

_____

_____

_____

_____

QUESTION 77.

(If You Could Trade Places With Anyone In The Department Of Corrections Who Would It Be, How Would You Obtain It, And Why?)

I would trade places with the superintend of corrections, so they can truly understand how people locked up are treated. I believe we truly don't understand things until we go through it our self, then our view of things change.

QUESTION 78.

(If You Could Switch Places With Any Race, What Race Would It Be And Why?)

I had to think about this question for a while, and I think that I would not want to switch places with another race, however I have thought about how it would be like to be treated the same as another race, and not hated for the race that I am.

QUESTION 79.

(What Is Your Biggest Desire?)

My biggest desire is to have at least 10 access, so I can build my mom a house, my twin brother a house, myself a house. Be that positive figure in the community that people in that community can count on.

_____

_____

_____

_____

_____

_____

_____

_____

_____

_____

_____

_____

_____

_____

_____

_____

_____

_____

_____

_____

QUESTION 80.

(Do You Have Any Sexual Fantasies?)

Yes, I do have sexual fantasies, I think we all do, some people just don't let them out. Seeing that I have been locked up most of my life, I haven't had the chance to act out some of my fantasies, however once I'm able, I will, we only live once right!

QUESTION 81.

(What Was The Most Terrifying Moment Of Your Life And Why?)

August of 1993, this year, I made the most terrifying mistake of my life. I did a robbery, two people lost their life this day by the hands of my brother and l. This will be some thing that will haunt me for the rest of my life.

_____

_____

_____

_____

_____

_____

_____

_____

_____

_____

_____

_____

_____

_____

_____

_____

_____

_____

_____

QUESTION 82.

(If You Could Go Back In Time, What Are The Things You Would Change?)

Being able to spend more time with my parents before losing them making better memories to help with the grieving process and hopefully helping grieving to get to a better place where memories can help bring smiles and tears if need be.

_____

_____

_____

_____

_____

_____

_____

_____

_____

_____

_____

_____

_____

_____

_____

_____

_____

QUESTION 83.

(Do You Have A Favorite Book That You Read Again And Again?)

The book that I can read over and over again is, "Nature Knows No Color Line" By. FA Rogers. This is a very good, historic book about history, he has wrote so many other good books as well.

QUESTION 84.

(What Is The Biggest Mistake Of Your Life?)

Doing my crime that brought me to prison. By me doing what I did to come to prison, not only hurt my victims family, but I also hurt, and let down my family as well. What hurts the most is, I had to grow up without my father, and I made a mistake, and my daughter had to grow up without me being in her life. I now make a vow that the males in this blood line stop coming to prison, it stops with me.

QUESTION 85.

(Who Was Your First Crush?)

My first crush was this girl named Kesha H. she lived right down the street from me when I lived in South Central Los California.

_____

_____

_____

_____

_____

_____

_____

_____

_____

_____

_____

_____

_____

_____

_____

_____

_____

_____

_____

_____

_____

QUESTION 86.

(What Is Your Most Valuable Possession And What Would You Do If You Lost It?)

I will say my mind is the most valuable possession, the knowledge that I have gained over my 41 years of life. Through all my trials and eras. If I lost this, I believe that I would loose my mental footing on the true meaning of living.

_____

_____

_____

_____

_____

_____

_____

_____

_____

_____

_____

_____

_____

_____

_____

_____

_____

_____

QUESTION 87.

(What Was Your New Years Resolution This Year And What Will It Be Next Year?)

Coming into this year 2019, the new years resolution that I set for my self, was to not let other peoples issues get me off my path, and become my issues. Two, deal with the things that I have the power to deal with, and let everything else go. Next year, I will wait until next year get here first!

QUESTION 88.

(What Makes You Laugh?)

What makes me laugh is the faces that people make. Like when they are shocked by what you said or when people don't expected something.

_____

_____

_____

_____

_____

_____

_____

_____

_____

_____

_____

_____

_____

_____

_____

_____

_____

_____

_____

QUESTION 89.

(If Your Soul Teleport Where Would You Go And Why?)

Because of where I am at in my life right now, I would like to teleport to my own island, where I could grow my own food and fruit. On the other part of the island would be like 10 to 15 people. Less people, less drama.

_____

_____

_____

_____

_____

_____

_____

_____

_____

_____

_____

_____

_____

_____

_____

_____

_____

_____

_____

_____

QUESTION 90.

(What Are Your Top Achievements?)

My top achievement would be my part t played in bringing my daughter into this world. She turned out very good. 2, me writing, and publishing my first book, more will come as well.

QUESTION 91.

(If You Had A Magic Gift What Would You Change In An Instance?)

I would change how people of color are viewed in this country. Looked upon as if we are less then. I would change the lack of education, bring it back to how education is first again. With education, comes awareness, with this comes incitement, and good change.

_____

_____

_____

_____

_____

_____

_____

_____

_____

_____

_____

_____

_____

_____

_____

_____

_____

_____

QUESTION 92.

(What Are Your Weaknesses?)

I find myself always being loyal to all the wrong people. I some time over think things, and I think myself out of position some times.

_____

_____

_____

_____

_____

_____

_____

_____

_____

_____

_____

_____

_____

_____

_____

_____

_____

QUESTION 93.

(What Are The Things You Can Say Yes To?)

People that seek knowledge/education. I can say yes, to being that one person that kids can look up to, and talk to no matter what!

QUESTION 94.

(What Are The Things You Can Say No To?)

People that's not willing to learn or change. I can say no, to all things that's not taking a step toward bettering self or others.

_____

_____

_____

_____

_____

_____

_____

_____

_____

_____

_____

_____

_____

_____

_____

_____

_____

_____

QUESTION 95.

(When Do You Feel Most Energized?)

I feel most energized when I have had at least 5 hours of sleep.

_____

_____

_____

_____

_____

_____

_____

_____

_____

_____

_____

_____

_____

_____

_____

_____

_____

_____

_____

_____

_____

_____

QUESTION 96.

(What Your Favorite Season And Why You Like It?)

I like the summer time because I'm more of a summer guy, I can work out, get myself in shape from the weight that I put on doing the winter.

_____

_____

_____

_____

_____

_____

_____

_____

_____

_____

_____

_____

_____

_____

_____

_____

_____

_____

_____

QUESTION 97.

(If You Had Magic Powers,
What Would That Be?)

I would like to be able to read or hear people's thoughts. This way, I would be able to reach every body on a level where they can understand, and truly understand that we all can make a change if we choose to.

QUESTION 98.

(How Do You See Your Life When You Are Older?)

I'm now in that older age bracket, I'm 41 years old now, I'm living my life, and what I want to do, and how I want to do, and how I want to give back to the community.

_____

_____

_____

_____

_____

_____

_____

_____

_____

_____

_____

_____

_____

_____

_____

_____

_____

QUESTION 99.

(What Is The Best Surprise You Ever Had In Your Life?)

The first one was when I was young and my mom told my twin brother and I that we was have a younger brother coming. I remember being so happy that I had a little brother coming to take care of. Then the second time I was surprised was when I found out that I was going to be a father.

QUESTION 100.

(What Are The Things That Stress You The Most?)

Being in prison, you have this since of helplessness all the time. Because most things are out of our control. On the outside things are always moving. When things come up with our loved once, we know if we where there things would be different, however we are not and this brings this sense of helplessness on.

_____

_____

_____

_____

_____

_____

_____

_____

_____

_____

_____

_____

_____

_____

_____

_____

QUESTION 101.

(What Are The Things That Remind You Of Your Childhood?)

The candy like nerds, or jaw breakers. The toys like the green machine, the green and black once with the big wheel in the front.

_____

_____

_____

_____

_____

_____

_____

_____

_____

_____

_____

_____

_____

_____

_____

_____

_____

_____

_____

QUESTION 102.

(If It Was Up To You, What Kind Of Person Would You Like For Our Next President To Be?)

I would like for it to be some one that could relate to every body a little. I would not mind seeing a woman president. I think with a woman in office, thing would be much different then what we have now or what we are use to.

_____

_____

_____

_____

_____

_____

_____

_____

_____

_____

_____

_____

_____

_____

_____

_____

QUESTION 103.

(What Is Your Ideal Outfit?)

I would say it really depends on what I'm trying to do in that moment. In special occasions, I would put on a suit, and tie.

_____

_____

_____

_____

_____

_____

_____

_____

_____

_____

_____

_____

_____

_____

_____

_____

_____

_____

_____

_____

QUESTION 104.

(What Are The Things You Really Want Right Now?)

I want my freedom back, so I can be the best son that I was put on this earth to be. I want the chance to be the best father that I was put on this earth to be to my beautiful daughter, and be the best gram father to my gram daughters, just be the best me.

_____

_____

_____

_____

_____

_____

_____

_____

_____

_____

_____

_____

_____

_____

_____

_____

_____

QUESTION 105.

(What Are The Things That Make You Safe?)

The things that make me safe are, knowing that I have people around me that I can count on, and fully trust in all situations.

_____

_____

_____

_____

_____

_____

_____

_____

_____

_____

_____

_____

_____

_____

_____

_____

_____

_____

_____

_____

_____

QUESTION 106.

(What Is The Meaning Of Life In Your Opinion?)

I believe we are all put on this earth for a reason, it's up to us to find out what this reason is. The meaning of life is special, life can be taken just as fast as it's given. This is why it's said, "as you live you make sure to do things to the fullest, as long as you give things your best, that's all you can do."

_____

_____

_____

_____

_____

_____

_____

_____

_____

_____

_____

_____

_____

_____

_____

_____

_____

QUESTION 107.

(Are You Scared Of Getting Old?)

I'm not scared of getting old, what I'm scared of is, as I get older, I will have pain in my body, then I will slow down and in my mind, I don't have time to stow down. So much time has already pasted me by because of me being in prison all my life.

QUESTION 108.

(What Are Your Earliest Memories?)

I was like 5 or 6 and we lived in Los Angeles and I was in the cub scouts down there. I remember the scout leaders taking us to a Los Angeles raiders game. This is when they played at the coliseum. This was the days.

_____

_____

_____

_____

_____

_____

_____

_____

_____

_____

_____

_____

_____

_____

_____

_____

_____

_____

_____

QUESTION 109.

(Do You Procrastinate About Anything?)

No I'm not a procrastinator, if I am doing this, it's because I did not want to be doing it anyway. I believe that life is to short to procrastinate or short change yourself or the people that's in your life.

_____

_____

_____

_____

_____

_____

_____

_____

_____

_____

_____

_____

_____

_____

_____

_____

_____

_____

_____

_____

QUESTION 110.

(Can You Go Naked On The Beach?)

Yes, I can go naked on the beach, I workout, I could work on my stomach a little more. However, if you feel good about yourself then that's all that matters.

_____

_____

_____

_____

_____

_____

_____

_____

_____

_____

_____

_____

_____

_____

_____

_____

_____

_____

_____

QUESTION 111.

(What Matters Most In Your Career?)

What matters most to me in my soon to be career, I want to be remembered for making people feel good. I want to be able to leave my hair business to my daughter, and my gran daughters.

QUESTION 112.

(Do You Masturbate And How?)

Yes, I masturbate, seeing that I have been in prison for some time now, I have mastered it. I believe you have to know and understand how to please yourself first before you can please anybody else.

_____

_____

_____

_____

_____

_____

_____

_____

_____

_____

_____

_____

_____

_____

_____

_____

_____

_____

_____

_____

QUESTION 113.

(How Do You Like To Sleep At Night, Naked Or With Clothes?)

I have tried sleeping without clothes and I did not like it at all. So I will sleep in my boxers at the least.

_____

_____

_____

_____

_____

_____

_____

_____

_____

_____

_____

_____

_____

_____

_____

_____

_____

_____

_____

_____

QUESTION 114.

(Do You Spend Too Much Time Doing Something That You Shouldn't?)

Now that I'm older, I try and make sure that everything that I do has purpose, and meaning. Because life is too short to not be doing the things that matter the most to you.

_____

_____

_____

_____

_____

_____

_____

_____

_____

_____

_____

_____

_____

_____

_____

_____

_____

_____

QUESTION 115.

(Is There Something That You Wish You Had More Time For?)

I wish that I had more time to spend with my family. Family is everything to me. Without family some type of way, shape or form. Life is just being, has no purpose, t would like to think that we all have purpose.

QUESTION 116.

(One Place You Wish You Could Go For The Holidays?)

I'm not sure right now, however I want to make sure that it's a place where all of my family could be there. I have never had the chance to be around all of my family at once.

_____

_____

_____

_____

_____

_____

_____

_____

_____

_____

_____

_____

_____

_____

_____

_____

_____

_____

QUESTION 117.

(What Are You Most Confident About?)

Doing hair, I know I'm good, and I braid hair fast. I know what I bring to the table in a friendship or a relationship. Knowing this has given me the most of most confidants.

QUESTION 118.

(What Are The Things You Like The Most With Your Mate?)

I am currently not with no body right now, however, I like a woman that's sure in what she wants, and needs. She is strong, outgoing, and is loyal. She will go above and beyond for her man because she will get that back from me.

_____

_____

_____

_____

_____

_____

_____

_____

_____

_____

_____

_____

_____

_____

_____

_____

_____

QUESTION 119.

(How Would You React If Someone Told You That You Were Ugly?)

I'm okay with me. I know that some people won't think that I'm good looking to them, and that's okay. I believe that there is someone out there for every body. You just have to find that some body that like you like you like them.

QUESTION 120.

(What Would You Do If You Were Locked Up In Your House For A Month?)

I would get all the cleaning done, I would make sure to do all the things that I have not had the chance to do.

_____

_____

_____

_____

_____

_____

_____

_____

_____

_____

_____

_____

_____

_____

_____

_____

_____

_____

_____

QUESTION 121.

(What Will You Do To Make Your Life More Meaningful?)

I will continue to reach out to those that are on the right path where they are ready to change their life, and they want to hear my story. I believe that once someone hear my story, I will touch their life in a good way. Now when I'm no longer on this earth, I hope that my life on this earth would have had some type of meaning.

_____

_____

_____

_____

_____

_____

_____

_____

_____

_____

_____

_____

_____

_____

_____

_____

_____

_____

QUESTION 122.

(Do You Believe You Can Be In Love With Two People At The Same Time?)

I have seen it done, and work, however I also believe that no matter what, you will love one person more than the other. Yes, I believe that you can love two people at the same time for different reasons.

_____

_____

_____

_____

_____

_____

_____

_____

_____

_____

_____

_____

_____

_____

_____

_____

_____

_____

_____

_____

Printed in the United States
by Baker & Taylor Publisher Services